Peas

by Kris Bonnell

Here is a pea seedling.

Pea seedlings grow into vines.

Flowers grow from the vines.

The flowers fall off and flat pea pods grow. Little peas are inside the pods.

The little peas grow into big peas.
The flat pea pods become fat pea pods!

9

Some peas are picked out
of the pods to eat.

Some peas grow
in the pod
for a long time.
They become pea seeds.

If pea seeds are planted,
they will grow.
The roots will grow.
The stem will grow.
The leaves will grow.

Peas grow and grow.

¿Voy ?

Por Mickey Daronco
Adaptado por Felicia López y Raquel C. Mireles

Está  .

lloviendo

Estoy en casa.

No voy
al  .

parque

No voy
a la .

playa

No voy al .

partido de pelota

Hago un .

rompecabezas

Estoy .

triste